T0128121

THE WILDERNESS

ENDURING GOD'S CALL TO WAIT

MARTY MCLAIN

WESTBOW
PRESS®
A DIVISION OF THOMAS NELSON
& ZONDERVAN

Scripture taken from the New King James Version®. Copyright © 1982 by Thomas Nelson. Used by permission. All rights reserved.

WestBow Press books may be ordered through booksellers or by contacting:

WestBow Press
A Division of Thomas Nelson & Zondervan
1663 Liberty Drive
Bloomington, IN 47403
www.westbowpress.com
1 (866) 928-1240

ISBN: 978-1-9736-1352-7 (sc)
ISBN: 978-1-9736-1353-4 (hc)
ISBN: 978-1-9736-1351-0 (e)

Library of Congress Control Number: 2018900286

Print information available on the last page.

WestBow Press rev. date: 01/31/2018

I would like to dedicate this book to my wife, Stephanie. Other than the Lord, you are my greatest joy in life. Your passion and faithfulness are without rival. You are my soulmate, lover, and best friend. I am glad we are "heirs together of the grace of life" (1 Peter 3:7).

Also, I would like to thank the leadership team of Summit Church. Your constant encouragement and support helped to sustain me when I was at my lowest. I will always be in your debt.

Finally, I would like to thank my oldest daughter, Virginia Greene, for all of the hard work you did to make this book possible. I don't think I could have done it without you.

INTRODUCTION

We had just moved into our new house in a growing suburb on the west side of Atlanta. The kids were enrolled in a new school, and my wife and I were excited about the future. All systems were full speed ahead. In that first week in our new residence, we had two unexpected visitors—a snake and a scorpion. That's right; within days of moving to the metropolitan capital of the south, I had to kill two creatures of the wild inside my home. I knew there was some biblical significance to the combination of a snake and a scorpion, but at the time I was too busy and life was too good for me to give it much consideration.

It wasn't until I was trying to put the pieces of my life back together that I gave serious thought to these encounters. Was God trying to give me a heads up that I was headed toward a wilderness experience? After all, Deuteronomy 8:15 speaks of snakes and scorpions as being part of the children of Israel's wilderness experience.

Whether God was preparing me or not, I can't definitively say. What I can say is that I did go into the wilderness, and what follows is a firsthand account of God's faithfulness.

Directionally Challenged

August 19, 1982, is a date that will live in infamy for those who are directionally challenged. It was on this day that major-league baseball pitcher Pascual Perez could not find his way to the Atlanta Fulton County Stadium to pitch for the Atlanta Braves. A native of the Dominican Republic, Perez was new to Atlanta, having recently been acquired in a trade with the Pittsburgh Pirates. It was his third home start for the Braves, but for some reason, he could not figure out how to get off the interstate.

Perez circled Atlanta several times on the I-285 perimeter before eventually getting off on the right exit.[1] Needless to say, he missed his start, and his circuitous route became indelibly etched into the memories of Braves fans everywhere.

Do you ever feel as though you are in the car with Pascual Perez? You are just driving around and can't get off on the right exit. You know that you have something very important you are supposed to do, but you just can't get to where you need to be. Even though you are trying your best to follow what you perceive is God's plan, you can't seem to find your way. You are trying to live right, to worship faithfully, and to give freely, but your life has gotten blown off course. I'm not talking about days or weeks. I'm talking about years. You do all the introspection, confession, and repentance you know to do, but still nothing changes. It seems

---

[1] Chris Jaffe, "30th Anniversary: Pascual Perez Circles the City of Atlanta. Repeatedly." August 19, 2012. http://www.hardballtimes.com/tht-live/30th-anniversary-pascual-perez-circles-atlanta.-repeatedly/.

as though God is watching you from afar and doing absolutely nothing to intervene.

As a man, how do you respond? You are supposed to be the strong one. How can you be strong for those you love when you feel abandoned by God?

Life-Altering Decision

In 2006, I was called to pastor a church that presented a lot of challenges. I was a relatively young man with a bright future. As such, I felt confident I could handle almost anything a church could throw at me. After all, I had been a pastor with a great track record over the past twelve years.

I was wrong. Call it hubris or whatever you like, but to make a long story short, I did not even make it a year. After eleven months, I resigned and began a long, strange ride that lasted a decade.

During this time, I struggled the most with the knowledge that prior to my resignation, I prayed immensely, sought godly counsel, and pored over scripture. I felt extremely confident that my bold actions were bathed in prayer and blessed by God.

Even though I felt like I followed God's will as best as I knew how, I wound up in a wilderness. How could I feel so confident and yet everything turned out so badly? I thought that I would be met with immediate success. With all the sincerity in my heart, I felt like I heard from God, and I acted accordingly.

So what happened? Was I that far off? To try to answer these questions, I began studying scripture to see if this had ever happened to anyone God had used. To both my delight and my distress, I discovered three stalwarts of the faith who also followed God's plan, and it led them to a place of waiting and hardship.

Blown Off Course but Not Off Purpose

Before I introduce these three biblical characters, I want to use an episode from the life of Jesus to illustrate how our lives can seemingly get blown off course. In Mark 6, Jesus had just fed five thousand people. We know from John 6 that in response to this miracle of biblical proportions, the people wanted to make Him king. However, Jesus quickly sent His disciples away in a boat and dispersed the crowd. He then spent some time in prayer by Himself up on a mountain.

With this background information in mind, I want to focus on what Jesus told the disciples to do. Scripture says, "Immediately He made His disciples get into the boat and go before Him to the other side, to Bethsaida" (Mark 6:45). While the disciples were crossing the water, they encountered an intense storm. The wind was blowing against them, and they were making no progress. As a matter of fact, the excursion turned into an all-night adventure. Somewhere between 3:00 and 6:00 a.m., as they were straining against the wind, the disciples saw what appeared to be a ghost and were terrified.

The figure in the storm was no ghost, but Jesus doing the impossible. He was walking on water. After speaking words of reassurance to His disciples, Jesus got into the boat with them.

We are told that soon after He got into the boat, the storm

ceased and the disciples were "greatly amazed" (Mark 6:51). However, the next part is very interesting.

A simple reading of the passage indicates that Jesus told His disciples to go to Bethsaida, but when they landed after the storm, they were at the "land of Gennesaret" (Mark 6:53). The storm had literally blown them off course. Even with Jesus in the boat, they didn't arrive where He told them to go. One writer comments, "The strong winds had sovereignly sent them to a different location."[2] Another writes, "Almost as an afterthought, Mark tells how far off course the disciples had been blown the night before."[3]

If the whole point of the story had been the disciples getting into the boat and sailing to Bethsaida, then they failed miserably because they didn't make it. If, however, it was about getting to know more about Jesus, then they succeeded. They witnessed the impossible. They saw Jesus walk on water. In this account, we learn that it was really about the experience and not the destination. The disciples may have been blown off course, but they still wound up where they needed to be. Confusing, isn't it?

In our day, men in particular need to be able to handle the unexpected events in life. I'm talking about the stuff that throws us off our game. You know, the sudden downturns and transitions of life that attack a man's inner sense of purpose. As a man, you must be able to gather yourself in the midst of the battle. As

---

[2] Daniel L. Akin, *Christ-Centered Exposition: Exalting Jesus in Mark* (Nashville, TN: B&H Publishing, 2013), 147.

[3] David L. McKenna, *The Preacher's Commentary Series*, Volume 25: Mark (Nashville, TN: Thomas Nelson, 1982), 141.

a leader, you have others who depend upon your strength and stability. You must stay the course.

Enduring Instead of Succeeding

When I resigned, I had no place to go. My plan was to start a new church in a town a few miles down the road. I knew the stakes were high. We had four kids and a mortgage. Feeling this enormous pressure, I recorded this prayer in my journal:

> I have been up since 4:00 this morning running everything through my mind. I tossed and I turned. If God doesn't do this church start thing, then I am sunk for years to come. I am out on a limb, but I feel like that is where I am supposed to be. The whole financial and logistical thing is hitting me like a ton of bricks. I need God's help. No one else's will do. I am in a desperate situation. All this can't help but to make me a better person, a better follower of Christ. God, please let my children see You come through in the midst of all this uncertainty. Please make Your way known.

This prayer kicked off a decade-long testing of my faith. Up to this time, I was used to seeing God come through in big ways in my life. I thought this new adventure of faith would be more of the same. I was wrong. This period was going to be the hardest decade of my existence. These prime years of life were going to be spent enduring instead of succeeding.

In the midst of the struggle, I had to make up my mind to stay the course. People were watching. My family needed me to be strong. If I went down, I knew I would take others with me. I had never felt so much pressure in my life. It's at times like this that an overused, yet motivating quote from Theodore Roosevelt really helps.

During his famous "Citizenship in a Republic" speech that he made in Paris, France, on April 23, 1909, the former president spoke these powerful words:

> It is not the critic who counts, not the man who points out how the strong man stumbles, or where the doer of deeds could have done them better. The credit belongs to the man who is actually in the arena, whose face is marred by dust and sweat and blood; who strives valiantly; who errs, and comes short again and again, because there is no effort without error and shortcomings; but who does actually strive to do the deeds; who knows the great enthusiasms, the great devotions; who spends himself in a worthy cause; who at the best knows in the end the triumph of high achievement, and who at the worst, if he fails, at least fails while daring greatly, so that his place

shall never be with those cold and timid souls who know neither victory or defeat.[4]

All I can say is that I went big!

A Biblical Pattern

Tough and unpredictable times are hard to handle. When a man is separated from what he perceives to be his God-given purpose, he is headed for a definite wilderness experience. Separation from purpose is about as bad as it gets for a man.

How do you endure? How do you make it for an extended period of time? I'm glad you asked. This little book discusses three biblical characters who overcame an extended period of being cut off from what they had been told was their God-given purpose.

Each of these three guys was given a promise from God concerning his future. Joseph had two dreams that one day he would rule over his family. The young shepherd boy, David, received word from the prophet Samuel that he would be the next king of Israel. The New Testament character Saul had an encounter with Jesus on the road to Damascus in which he was told that he would proclaim the name of Jesus before Gentiles, kings, and the children of Israel.

In each case, the fulfillment of God's word came through much conflict and waiting. The path to fulfillment was long and

[4] http://www.leadershipnow.com/leadingblog/2010/04/theodore_roosevelts_the_man_in.html

treacherous. It took incredible perseverance and the goodness of God for each one to see God's promises come true. These men serve as our examples.

Maybe you can identify with Joseph. You do your best, but there is no chance for a promotion. All you can do is wait and remain faithful. Perhaps David is your hero, and like him, you only fight to live another day. You aren't really trying to get ahead; you're just trying to survive. It could be that you are like Saul, who eventually became known as Paul. You labor away in obscurity while losing everything on which you built your life—wealth, family, and friends. You aren't losing them because you are doing wrong; you are losing them because you are trying to do right.

Whichever example you identify with, it all comes to the same point. When you see no light at the end of the tunnel, your only hope is divine intervention.

Can you hold on? Can you do your best when there is no chance of promotion? Can you fight to live another day? Can you live in obscurity while all you have achieved in life is jerked out from under you?

I hope that you answered yes to all of these questions because with God's strength, you can do it. Sometimes it's not about getting from point A to point B but about getting to know Jesus better. It's about preparing for what God wants you to do. So, let's delve into the lives of Joseph, David, and Paul and draw strength from their examples for the journey God has you on.

PART I

Joseph

Letting Adversity Prepare You for Success

CHAPTER 1

Overcoming Hardship

It is incredible what people can overcome in life. Take, for instance, George Washington Carver. His life story is nothing short of amazing. Carver was born into slavery in 1864 in Diamond, Missouri. As if that were not a bad enough start in life, Carver was kidnapped along with his mother and sister when he was only a week old and taken to Kentucky, where he was resold into slavery. Fortunately for the young George, he was recovered by an agent who worked for his previous owner and returned to Missouri.[5] After his emancipation at the conclusion of the Civil War, Carver's master, Moses Carver, and his wife, Sarah, decided to raise George and his brother as their foster sons.[6] The young

[5] "George Washington Carver Biography," Biography.com. 2016. http://www.biography.com/people/george-washington-carver-9240299#early-years.
[6] Linda O. McMurray, "George Washington Carver," The Reader's Companion to American History, 1991. http://www.history.com/topics/black-history/george-washington-carver.

man who was born a slave, stolen, and resold into slavery was now an adopted son.

As a child, George had an insatiable appetite for learning. This desire led him to go wherever a young black man in that time could go in order to further his education. A series of twists and turns led Carver to Iowa, where he was able to fulfill his educational pursuits. Through hard work and determination, he became one of the top scientists of his day.

Eventually Carver became one of President Theodore Roosevelt's go-to guys on issues regarding agriculture.[7] Among many other awards, Carver was inducted into the British Royal Society of Arts. His fame was so widespread that even notorious bad guy Joseph Stalin sought Carver's agricultural expertise in the USSR.[8] Carver, however, declined the invitation.

Perhaps his most endearing contribution was the development of over three hundred products from the peanut.[9] Without a doubt, George Washington Carver was a brilliant man. Born with little chance for success, all he needed was an opportunity, and when he got it, he made the world a better place.

---

[7] "Famous African American Inventors," Culture and Change: Black History in America, 2016. http://www.teacher.scholastic.com/activities/bhistory/inventors/carver.htm.

[8] "George Washington Carver: American Agricultural Chemist," Encyclopedia Britannica, June 22, 2015. http://www.britannica.com/biography/George-Washington-Carver.

[9] Mary Bagley, "George Washington Carver: Biography, Inventions and Quotes," LiveScience, December 6, 2013. http://www.livescience.com/41780-george-washington-carver.html.

Dreams of Greatness

History tells us of others who made the most of their opportunities. For some it was a one-time shot. These chosen people of history had to be ready when that moment came. Perhaps no one in the Bible had more at stake in a one-time shot than Joseph of the Old Testament. After thirteen years as a slave and prisoner, his opportunity for freedom came unexpectedly, and he had to be ready. In order to understand his long odds, you need to know Joseph's backstory.

The account begins in Genesis 37. Joseph was the favorite son of the patriarch Jacob. His mother, Rachel, was Jacob's favorite wife. This is important to note because Jacob had four wives. As you can imagine, there was a lot of bad blood between Joseph and his brothers. This rivalry only intensified because Jacob showed overt favoritism to Joseph. When a father favors one son over his siblings, the resentment can turn ugly. That's what happened to Joseph.

When Joseph was seventeen, he was tending sheep with some of his brothers. During the course of fulfilling their shepherding responsibilities, the brothers did something pretty bad. We are not told what they did, but we are told that Joseph reported their misdeeds to his father.[10]

Here we have the classic case of a tattletale. To top it off, scripture says that Jacob loved Joseph more than any of his other sons and that, as a sign of this greater love, he made Joseph a robe of many colors. The bestowal of the coat solidified the brothers'

---

[10] See Gen. 37:2–4.

hatred for Joseph. This hatred was so intense that scripture says they "could not speak peaceably to him" (Genesis 37:4). They loathed their little brother.

Not only was Joseph his daddy's favorite, but he also had dreams that prophesied he would one day rule over his brothers. His first dream involved a sheaf of wheat standing tall and other sheaves bowing down to it. The tall sheaf represented Joseph, and the sheaves bowing down represented his brothers. Just what kind of reaction could Joseph expect from his brothers? Scripture says that "they hated him even more."[11]

Joseph had another dream that he told his family, which involved the sun, moon, and eleven stars bowing down to him. This was a little too much for even his father. Jacob rebuked Joseph and said, "What is this dream that you have dreamed? Shall your mother and I and your brothers indeed come to bow down to the earth before you?" (Genesis 37:10). As you can imagine, this dream only made the brothers even more jealous of Joseph.

Walking Off a Cliff

A few months before my ordeal began, I remember driving around one day and getting a phone call from the town where I had previously pastored. On the other end of the phone was a lady I did not know. She began the conversation by telling me that I probably did not know her, but she knew me, and there was something that she really needed to tell me. In an almost

---

[11] See Gen. 37:8.

apologetic way, she began describing to me that the Lord would not let her rest until she called me and told me what she was about to say.

As you can imagine, she had my attention. She told me that she had a dream that I was about to walk off a cliff, but I was going to be all right. By her own admission, she was embarrassed to call me and she felt a little foolish, but she could get no peace until she did. So, I thanked her for her call, and I immediately thought that the whole conversation was very strange.

At the time, everything in my life was great. Everybody loved me, and the future looked fantastic. It was only after the wheels fell off that I remembered the conversation. To this day, I still do not know the woman's identity, but I would prefer that people not have dreams of me walking off a cliff.

The Tipping Point

Returning to the story in Genesis, the situation involving Joseph came to a head when Jacob sent him to check on his brothers, who could not be trusted. At this time, the brothers were supposed to be with their flock in Shechem, but when Joseph arrived, they were nowhere to be found. Instead, for whatever reason, they were in Dothan. When Joseph found his brothers and approached them, they began to plot against him. They wanted to kill the sibling given to delusional dreams.

This was going to be a premeditated murder, a fratricide in the tradition of Cain and Abel. Fortunately for Joseph, his oldest brother, Rueben, talked the angry brothers out of killing him and instead put him in a pit. Rueben's plan was to come back and rescue Joseph later.

When Joseph got within reach of his brothers, they disrobed him and threw him into the pit. As Joseph begged for help, his brothers sat down to enjoy a meal. While they were eating, a caravan of Ishmaelites passed by on their way to Egypt. The brothers came up with the idea that instead of killing Joseph and having nothing to show for it, they could sell him and make some money. So they agreed to sell him to the Ishmaelite traders for twenty shekels of silver.

To cover up their crime, the brothers dipped Joseph's tunic in the blood of a goat, and when they arrived home, they told their father that a wild animal had eaten him. All that was left was a bloody remnant of his coat of many colors. As expected, Jacob mourned greatly over the loss of his favorite son.

The Downward Spiral

The next part of Joseph's story focuses on his downward spiral of fortune. Midianite traders sold him to Potiphar, the captain of the guard for Pharaoh, when he was seventeen years of age. He had gone from being the favored son in a large family to a slave in a foreign country. How could God allow this to happen?

God was aware of what was going on in Joseph's life. As Joseph began his life of slavery in Egypt, the Bible says that the Lord made everything Joseph did prosper (Genesis 39:3). Because of Joseph's abilities, Potiphar even put him in charge of his entire household.

It appears that Joseph was making the best of a bad situation. God blessed his life in an extraordinary fashion. However, a soap opera soon followed.

Joseph was a good-looking guy, and Potiphar's wife was a woman on the prowl. Scripture says, "And it came to pass after these things that his master's wife cast longing eyes on Joseph, and she said, 'Lie with me'" (Genesis 39:7). She was not suggesting a nap.

Joseph refused her adulterous advances by citing Potiphar's trust in him and his own desire not to sin against God, but the woman would not relent. Finally, when no one else was in the house, she seized Joseph and told him to lie with her. Joseph's response was a godly one: he ran! He escaped her advances but not her wrath. The old saying that "hell hath no fury like a woman scorned" is true. Because of his rejection of her, Potiphar's wife screamed and then accused Joseph of trying to rape her. Potiphar angrily threw him into the dungeon where the king's prisoners were held.

Once again, we might wonder how God could allow this to happen. Here was a guy who was making the best of a bad situation, and he got hammered a second time. It's as though he kept sinking lower and lower. However, the Bible says that "the Lord was with Joseph and showed him mercy, and He gave him favor in the sight of the keeper of the prison" (Genesis 39:21).

God continued to give Joseph favor with others, but the situations kept getting worse. The biblical story is framed in such a way as to make the first-time reader believe that Joseph was a young man whom God was going to use greatly. Everything up to this point, though, tells a different story.

Joseph seems like a walking billboard for Murphy's Law.[12] He also reminds one of the poster for a missing dog that reads, "Lost dog, blind in right eye, missing one leg, tail broken, recently castrated, answers to the name of Lucky."[13] Scripture says that God was with Joseph, but at this point in his life, it didn't appear so.

From Boy Slave to Patron Saint

In the fifth century, a sixteen-year-old British boy named Patrick was kidnapped by raiders and sold into slavery in Ireland, where he lived as a slave for the next six years. One night he had a dream in which a voice told him that a ship would be waiting for him the next day to take him to freedom.[14] The next morning Patrick was able to board an offshore boat to return home to Britain. For the next twenty-six years, Patrick served as a priest.

At the age of forty-eight, he had another life-altering dream. This time he felt compelled to return to the land of his captivity as a missionary.[15] Thus, the future patron saint of Ireland began his improbable ministry to his former captors.

He was so successful that many countries honor him with a special day on their calendars. In America, we celebrate him with a big parade in New York City. As a matter of fact, in some circles when you fail to honor Saint Patrick by not wearing green, you

---

[12] http://www.dictionary.com/browse/murphy-s-law.

[13] http://www.ebay.com/itm/350944482844

[14] George G. Hunter III, *The Celtic Way of Evangelism* (Nashville, TN: Abington Press, 2000), 14.

[15] Ibid., 15.

might get pinched. All this later fame was the result of his life being shaped by two dreams. Joseph also had dreams, but his thus far had led only to enslavement.

The Saga Continues

Let's fast-forward in the story of Joseph's life. It has now been over ten years since Joseph's brothers sold him into slavery. He has gone from being a household slave in Potiphar's mansion to being a prisoner in a dungeon. Little did Joseph know that he was about to rub shoulders with some very important people.

For some unknown reason, Pharaoh had become dissatisfied with his butler and baker. They were both thrown into prison, where they awaited their fate. One night, the butler and baker had dreams. When Joseph saw them the next morning, he could tell that they were troubled. When they told him about their dreams, Joseph interpreted them.

According to the dreams, the baker was going to have his head cut off by Pharaoh, and the butler was going to be restored to his previous position. As Joseph interpreted the butler's dream, he asked, "Remember me when it is well with you, and please show kindness to me; make mention of me to Pharaoh, and get me out of this house. For indeed I was stolen away from the land of the Hebrews; and also I have done nothing here that they should put me into the dungeon" (Gen. 40:14–15).

Three days later, Joseph's interpretation came to pass. The baker's head was cut off, and the butler's position was restored.

However, when the butler was released from the dungeon, he immediately forgot about Joseph.

Forgotten

On January 25, 1998, an Australian charter boat forgot two American tourists, Tom and Eileen Lonergan, after a diving expedition. The boat, *Outer Edge*, was forty miles off the coast of Australia at the Great Barrier Reef.[16] The crew thought that all the divers had surfaced, but they failed to take a head count. It wasn't until two days later that the charter company realized their terrible mistake.[17]

In spite of an extensive search effort, no human remains were found. However, a local fisherman recovered the Lonergans' scuba equipment and a dive slate. The dive slate had these chilling words scrawled on it: "Monday, Jan. 26, 1998, 08 a.m. To anyone [who] can help us: We have been abandoned on A[gin]court Reef by MV *Outer Edge* 25 Jan. 98, 3 p.m. Please [come] to rescue us before we die. Help!!!"[18]

Imagine being left in one of the most shark-infested parts of

---

[16] David Fickling, "The Cruel Sea," *The Guardian*, July 22, 2004. http://www.theguardian.com/film/2004/jul/23/2.

[17] Robert Milikin, "Divers Inquest Points to Sharks," *Independent*, September 10, 1998. http://www.independent.co.uk/news/divers-inquest-points-to-sharks-1197328.html.

[18] Fickling, "The Cruel Sea." https://www.theguardian.com/film/2004/jul/23/2.

the ocean with no help. It is never a pleasant experience when we are forgotten, especially when the stakes are so high.

Didn't Know You Were Still Around

Perhaps you feel forgotten. Life has passed you by, and you are not even in the rearview mirror. At one time, I had good standing in our denomination. I had been asked to serve on several state committees and even a national one. Several years into my ordeal, I went back to our state denominational headquarters to meet with someone. As I waited for the elevator, a well-known state leader got off, and we saw each other. I will never forget what he said.

"Marty, I didn't know you were still around."

Ouch! That hurt. At the time, I was feeling really small. After this interaction, I was microscopic.

God Can Make People Remember You

If the story ended with Joseph living out the rest of his life in prison, it would be tragic. It would all have been a bad joke. However, God has a way of getting the attention of the powerful in order to make them act in ways that fulfill His plan. It's a recurrent theme in scripture.

In the book of Esther, the Persian king Xerxes developed a bad case of insomnia. He decided to read the realm's chronicles in order to go to sleep. As he did so, Xerxes discovered that honor had never been shown to a Jew who had saved his life from a potential coup. This man's name was Mordecai.

It just so happened that the king's remembrance occurred at a pivotal moment in Jewish history. At this time, a powerful Persian official named Haman had just hatched a plot to have all of the Jews in the empire put to death. The king's remembrance of Mordecai triggered a string of events that saved the Jews from extinction. Mordecai and his niece, Esther, subverted Haman's plans and expanded the power of the Jews in the empire.

All of this happened because at the right time, a pagan king remembered to honor a Jew who had saved his life. It was a God thing. The next part of Joseph's story was also a God thing.

CHAPTER 2

Living the Dream

Two years after the butler left the dungeon, something occurred that changed Joseph's life. Pharaoh had a dream that no one could interpret—not even the magicians or wise men in all of Egypt. It was at this time that Pharaoh's butler remembered Joseph. He told Pharaoh about his experience with Joseph and how he had correctly interpreted a dream years earlier.

Upon hearing the butler's testimonial, Pharaoh immediately sent his guards to get Joseph out of the dungeon. Joseph was cleaned up and given some new clothes before being whisked into the presence of Pharaoh.

Pharaoh then recounted his dream to Joseph. When Joseph was given the opportunity to speak, he was quick to give God the glory for any correct interpretation.

Pharaoh's dream involved seven thin cows eating seven fat cows. In addition, Pharaoh saw seven full heads of grain being devoured by seven meager heads of grain. Joseph told Pharaoh that the dream meant seven years of plenty followed by seven years of famine. God was giving Pharaoh a heads-up so he could make provision for the coming famine in Egypt.

Joseph then instructed Pharaoh to put someone in charge of storing up food during those seven years of plenty. He specifically advised putting aside one-fifth of the harvest every year during the time of plenty to prepare for the time of famine. Pharaoh was so impressed by the plan that he appointed Joseph to the position of second-in-command over all of Egypt. Joseph was thus given the authority to implement his plan. As an outward sign of his esteem, Pharaoh gave Joseph a royal robe, a gold chain, and his signet ring. And to top it all off, he even arranged for Joseph's marriage.

All of a sudden, everything had changed. In one day, Joseph went from the dungeon to the palace. For thirteen years he had languished away as a household slave and then as a prisoner. As a slave and prisoner, Joseph had no idea of what his future held, but when it was time for the Lord to use him, he was ready. Joseph kept his heart pure and his mind sharp. He did not cast away restraint because of discouragement and feelings of abandonment. Instead, he lived with faith and integrity.

Because of his unwavering commitment to God, he learned the correct interpretation of Pharaoh's dream. Everything depended upon being ready for that unexpected moment. He didn't know what would happen or when it would happen. He simply trusted in a God he could not see.

As the rest of the book of Genesis unfolds, we see that what was going on in Joseph's life was about a lot more than Joseph. It was about God's overarching plan for His people.

During the next fourteen years of feast and famine, Joseph greatly extended the power of Pharaoh. Starving people from all over the region came to Egypt looking for food. Joseph brokered deals that enhanced Pharaoh's power and wealth. He was Pharaoh's greatest asset.

The severe famine also extended into the land of Canaan, where Joseph's father and brothers lived with their families. Eventually they too came seeking food from Egypt.

Revenge or Reconciliation

There is a popular saying that revenge is a dish best served cold. The understood meaning is that revenge is the most satisfying when it happens long after the original cause occurred.[19] Unexpected payback is the best, or at least that is what the saying implies.

At this point in Joseph's life, it had been over twenty years since his brothers sold him into slavery. So when the brothers arrived in Egypt looking for food, it would have been understandable for Joseph to react in anger. After all, isn't payback the stuff of great movies?

Whether it's Clint Eastwood in *The Outlaw Josey Wells,* Jim Caviezel in *The Count of Monte Cristo,* or Leonardo DiCaprio in *The Revenant,* Hollywood has a way of exalting revenge. Therefore, a first-time reader might expect Joseph to have some revenge up his sleeve.

---

[19] Oxford Dictionaries online. http://www.oxforddictionaries.com/us/definition/american_english/revenge-is-a-dish-best-served-or-eaten-cold.

Joseph's response, however, is unexpected. He wept. He was not a bitter man filled with unforgiveness. He had not spent the last twenty years plotting his revenge. His life had been lived for God's purposes and not his own. If his only reason for living was to get back at his brothers, there would have been nothing left to live for once his revenge had been exacted.

Revenge is indeed a powerful motivator but a terrible companion. You don't want to be like Inigo Montoya in *The Princess Bride* who, when he was finally able to exact revenge on the six-fingered man who killed his father, said, "You know, it's very strange. I have been in the revenge business so long, now that it's over, I don't know what to do with the rest of my life."[20]

Joseph wanted complete reconciliation with his brothers. This could not happen until his brothers were willing to acknowledge their previous crime against him. Instead of exacting revenge, Joseph sought to bring his brothers to repentance and reconciliation.

When they first saw him in Egypt after many years of separation, they did not recognize him. They thought he was just some high-ranking Egyptian official. Through an elaborate series of events, the brothers came to grips with their sinful treatment of Joseph. When Joseph was assured of the depth of their repentance, he then revealed his true identity to them. As they stood in stunned silence, he assured them of his forgiveness and love. Joseph realized it was all part of God's plan.

After Joseph revealed himself to his brothers, he invited them and their families to live with him in Egypt. Pharaoh offered them

---

[20] http://www.princessbride.8m.com/script.htm.

the fertile land of Goshen. God's sovereign plan was unfolding. The Jewish people were intact and lived in Egypt for the next four hundred years.

Years later when his father Jacob died, Joseph's brothers feared a reprisal from Joseph, but their fears were completely unfounded. As a matter of fact, revenge was nowhere in Joseph's heart. He viewed the difficult events that had transpired in his life as part of a bigger picture that God was painting. He told his brothers, "Do not be afraid, for am I in the place of God? But as for you, you meant evil against me; but God meant it for good, in order to bring it about as it is this day, to save many people alive. Now therefore, do not be afraid; I will provide for you and your little ones" (Gen. 50:19–21).

Everything that Joseph endured was for a greater purpose. He knew his brothers meant evil against him, but he also knew that God's plan was greater than man's misdeeds. Joseph's years in slavery translated into lives being saved from starvation. God does indeed work all things together for good!

Others Gain from Your Pain

When I was contemplating resigning from the church I pastored, I found a book that intrigued me. It was titled *Don't Waste Your Life*. Of course, this book written by John Piper is now considered a classic. However, I had never heard of it until I saw it in a bookstore while on vacation. The book became my steady companion for my week's stay at the beach.

I was captivated by the thought that I was going to waste my life in an impossible situation. As a matter of fact, I often used the word *untenable* to describe my current pastorate. I did not want to be like the couple in the book that took early retirement to sail the seas and collect seashells and to play softball.[21]

I was taking a huge risk if I resigned my church and started a new one. I could have put out a resume and gone to another church, but I had three teenage children at the time, and to uproot them so quickly at that stage of life could have had devastating effects. Another option was to just stay where I was and keep my mouth shut and be a company guy, but like the book challenged, I didn't want to waste my life.

Perhaps the most motivating quote in Piper's book is about the price to be paid when we choose not to act in faith.

> What if circumstances are such that not taking a risk will result in loss and injury? It may not be wise to play it safe. And what if a successful risk would bring great benefit to many people, and its failure would bring harm only to yourself? It may not be loving to choose comfort or security when something great may be achieved for the cause of Christ and for the good of others.[22]

I can testify that what I did brought much good into a lot of people's lives. My children prospered and our new church helped a lot of people through difficult times. However, I personally went

---

[21] John Piper, *Don't Waste Your Life* (Wheaton, IL: Crossway 2003), 47.
[22] Ibid., 80.

way down. What should have been the most productive years of ministry were actually my least productive. The phrase "the lost decade" is often used to refer to Japan's economic woes of the 1990s. I use it to refer to the ten years after I resigned.

My personal influence waned greatly. My opportunities turned into a trickle. I suffered, but others were put in a position to excel. God was glorified but just not in the way I thought He would be. Oh, and by the way, I threw Piper's book into the garbage.

Putting It All Together

Joseph's future was dependent on events totally beyond his control. Humanly speaking, he needed the help of other people to get out of the dungeon. He could not do it himself. His freedom was in the hands of others. When the time was right, God orchestrated the circumstances for others to liberate Joseph.

Are you willing to wait for God to orchestrate events in your life to achieve His purpose?

While Joseph waited, he did what was right in the sight of the Lord. There's something to be said for continuing to do your best even when it seems that it does not matter. Joseph had every opportunity to give up, but he didn't. When he was a slave in the household of Potiphar, he was the best slave in the house. When he was a prisoner in the king's dungeon, he was the best prisoner in the dungeon. Colossians 3:23–24 says, "And whatever you do, do it heartily, as to the Lord and not to men, knowing that from the Lord you will receive the reward of the inheritance; for you serve the Lord Christ."

Joseph chose to keep a sharp mind and a pure heart even when it seemed as though the circumstances of his life would never change. If he was asked about his goals in life, he probably would have given a simple answer: "Get out of this dungeon." That's it. No John Maxwell stuff on vision or anything like that. He just wanted his freedom from what seemed like a hopeless situation.

If you feel as though the outward circumstances of your life are beyond your control, continue to do your best for God.

Are you willing to continue to do your best even when it seems as though it really doesn't matter?

Joseph also had a lot of emotional stuff to overcome. He was betrayed by his brothers and sold into slavery. His boss's wife falsely accused him of attempted rape. The butler forgot him when he was in the dungeon. Being betrayed, falsely accused, and forgotten is a lot of emotional stuff to have to deal with. But Joseph never let unforgiveness and bitterness dominate his life.

At the end of the story, we see how he chose forgiveness over retribution. Joseph told his brothers these words when they expressed their fear that he would seek revenge once their father had passed away: "But as for you, you meant evil against me; but God meant it for good, in order to bring it about as it is this day, to save many people alive" (Gen. 50:20).

Joseph looked at the bigger picture of what God was doing in the world. He viewed the events of his life as being orchestrated by God for a greater purpose. Because he was a big-picture guy, Joseph was able to forgive those who had wronged him.

Are you letting the emotional pain of the past prevent you from living life to the fullest in the present?

Repositioned for Impact

Sometimes God uses the strangest series of events to position our lives for maximum impact for His kingdom. This repositioning may occur because of God's chastening in our lives, or it may be through no fault of our own. Regardless of the cause, God is the one who controls the flow of history.

Take, for instance, Psalm 126. This psalm recounts the children of Israel's sudden release from Babylonian captivity. Previously, God judged the nation because of their idolatry and their obstinance to His Word. Because of their continued disobedience, they suffered a series of three defeats at the hands of the Babylonian Empire. After each defeat, captives were taken away to Babylon.

In 605 BC, Daniel and his three Hebrew friends, Shadrach, Meshach, and Abednego, were taken away. In 597, Ezekiel the prophet and others were taken to Babylon. Finally, in 586 the last group of captives was exiled to Babylon and the city of Jerusalem with its temple, and its wall was destroyed.

In exile, the Jews received a letter from Jeremiah the prophet telling them to build houses in Babylon and to plant vineyards because they were going to be there until the seventy years of Babylonian supremacy was complete. As a reminder of God's purpose, He included the famous words from Jeremiah 29:11, "For I know the thoughts that I think toward you, says the Lord, thoughts of peace and not of evil, to give you a future and a hope." In other words, He was telling them to make the best life they could where they were, because their prayers to return to the promised land would not be answered until the time was complete.

God had to reposition the Jews. His original design for the Jewish nation was for them to be a light to the surrounding Gentile nations. It would be through Israel that the Gentiles would see how God was to be worshipped. The children of Israel were to be God's light to a dark world. When they ceased to fulfill His purpose, God had to discipline them to reposition them to impact the world.

Suddenly, in 539 BC with little warning, the Medes and the Persians captured Babylon in a daring nighttime maneuver. With this defeat, the time of the Babylonians came to a screeching halt. The new Persian king, Cyrus, issued a decree that allowed the Jews to return to their homeland. Furthermore, he commanded funds to be taken out of the king's treasury in order to pay for them to rebuild the temple in Jerusalem.

This dramatic turn of events is why the psalm speaks of the people being in utter amazement. Even the Gentiles said, "The Lord has done great things for them" (Psalm 126:2). The Jews agreed in verse 3, "The Lord has done great things for us, and we are glad." What a tremendous testimony. Even the Gentile nations who did not worship the true God had to confess that the God of the Jews had done a great work on their behalf. Once again, light shone through God's people.

The Bible reminds us that God has a purpose for our lives. We are told in scripture that we are God's workmanship (Ephesians 2:10), His living epistles (2 Cor. 3:3), His ambassadors (2 Cor. 5:20), and His witnesses (Acts 1:8). God has a story that He wants to tell the world through our lives. This story is about who He is and how He can be known.

We must be faithful to live life in a God-honoring way, even when we feel as though we are in exile. It is during these trying times that God is positioning our lives for greater impact for His kingdom. Through the experiences of our lives, He is communicating who He is to the world. Pray big and be patient. Ask God to do what only He can do, and then be willing to work hard to do what He expects you to do. It is through this joining together of God's sovereignty and our hard work that we experience the magnificence of His plan.

Part II

David

The Perils of Early Success When Followed by Hardship

CHAPTER 3

Navigating the Success-
Failure Pendulum

Comparison and contrast is a good tool for learning. You can gain a lot of knowledge by studying the successes and failures of others. For instance, it is interesting to study child actors as they move forward in their lives. Some succeed while others crash and burn.

Consider two childhood actors from the 1960s and early 1970s. Ron Howard starred as Opie Taylor in *The Andy Griffith Show* and Danny Bonaduce played the role of Danny in *The Partridge Family*. These two redheads experienced widespread popularity as adolescent television stars. However, after early stardom, their paths went in opposite directions. Howard went on to future acting success in *American Graffiti* and *Happy Days* while Bonaduce was not so fortunate. After the Partridge Family was cancelled, Bonaduce spent time living on the streets. By his own admission he was "homeless in Hollywood."[23]

As the years unfolded, Howard became a successful Hollywood director. One of his movies, *The Cinderella Man,* was even nominated for an Academy Award. Instead of making news by directing an inspiring boxing movie, Bonaduce made news by engaging in a celebrity boxing match with fellow childhood star Donny Osmond. Bonaduce won the profanity-laced match by a split decision. Afterward, a childish argument ensued in which Bonaduce called Osmond a woman and told him to "Go fight with Marie."[24] So much for inspiring others.

Bonaduce subsequently wrote a book titled *Random Acts of Badness* in which he told of his slide into a destructive lifestyle. *Publishers Weekly* began its review of Bonaduce's book with these words: "Bonaduce is primarily known for two things: costarring as red-headed Danny on TV's *The Partridge Family* from 1970 to 1974 and his downward spiral into drug addiction, culminating in his arrest for assaulting a transvestite prostitute in Arizona."[25]

Conversely, the book written on Howard's life was titled *From Mayberry to the Moon and Beyond.* One reviewer summarized it

---

[23] http://www.dailymail.co.uk/news/article-2384677/Danny-Bonaduce-Former-Partridge-Family-child-star-says-lived-car-near-Walk-Fame-ended.html

[24] Dennis Polkow, "Boys Will Be Boys: Bonaduce Wins a Donnybrook," *Chicago Tribune,* January 18, 1994. http://www.articles.chicagotribune.com/1994-01-18/news/9401180139_1_donny-osmond-ring-danny-bonaduce.

[25] Review of *Random Acts of Badness: My Story, Publishers Weekly,* www.publishersweekly.com/978-0-7868-6722-6.

with these heart-warming words: "In a way, Howard's rise from fading child actor to distinguished director isn't a Hollywood tale at all. It's the story of the triumph of rock-solid American values over Glitter Gulch glitz. The book is a terrific read with a grand finale. In the end, Opie grows up. And turns into Ron Howard."[26] Howard is heralded as being successful throughout all phases of his career, whereas Bonaduce is known for having a hard time just staying on the right side of the law.

It goes without saying that early success can be hard to overcome later in life. The biblical character David is a great example of someone who succeeded early in life and then was able to skillfully navigate a downturn in fortune to emerge once again poised for success. In the process, he had to demonstrate an incredible combination of courage and restraint to follow God's plan.

The Renaissance Man

David is perhaps the best-known character of the Old Testament. He was the shepherd boy who became king. He is the one referred to as a man after God's own heart, yet he became a murderer and an adulterer. His encounter with Goliath is the classic story about an underdog coming out on top.

David was a Renaissance man before there was a Renaissance. He led men in battle and then went home to play his harp. He was adept with a slingshot as well as a pen. He was the heartthrob of

---

[26] Beverly Gray, "The Book," http://www.beverlygray.com/ron-howard.php.

all the young ladies, and on top of that, he could dance. He was that guy. However, his ascension to power proved very difficult.

At times, it looked as though it simply would not happen. In order to appreciate all that David had to endure before he experienced the fulfillment of God's promise, we need to start from the beginning.

Underdog Hero

It's interesting how some people get unexpected opportunities. One of my favorite movies of all time is *Rocky*, the story of a two-bit boxer who is given a chance to fight for the world championship. You probably know the plot. Apollo Creed, the reigning champion, was looking for a replacement to fight him on January 1, 1976, when his original opponent was injured. Because it was the year of America's bicentennial, Apollo wanted to find an opponent who was significant in terms of the nation's anniversary.

After sifting through potential challengers, Apollo chose Rocky Balboa and gave the rationale for his unexpected choice: "Look, it's the name, man. The Italian Stallion. The media will eat it up. Now who discovered America? An Italian, right? What better way to get it on than with one of its descendants?"[27] Thus, Rocky was given an unexpected opportunity, and the rest was history (or in this case, a series of sequels spanning four decades).

---

[27] "Quotes for Apollo Creed," IMDb.com, http://www.imdb.com/character/ch0002253/quotes.

The Rise of a Shepherd Boy

In 1 Samuel, we read of a Jewish teenager who was unexpectedly selected by God to be the next king of Israel. David was the youngest of the sons of Jesse and lived during the time of Israel's first monarch. King Saul was a colossal disappointment. His failures were so great that God told the prophet Samuel to go to Jesse's house and anoint the young man who would become Israel's next king. Of course, all of this had to be done secretively because Samuel would have been put to death if Saul knew he was anointing another king.

In obedience to God, Samuel went to Jesse's house and asked to see his sons. Jesse had all of his older sons parade before Samuel, but God had chosen none of them. Samuel expected an impressive specimen similar to Saul, who was handsome and tall. Instead, God told the prophet, "Do not look at his appearance or his physical stature … For the Lord does not see as man sees; for man looks at the outward appearance, but the Lord looks at the heart" (1 Sam. 16:7).

In desperation, Samuel asked Jesse if he had any more sons. There was one left, the youngest, who was out tending sheep.

When David entered the room, the Bible describes him as ruddy and handsome. These are not necessarily qualities that one looks for in a warrior king, but God spoke to Samuel and said, "Arise, anoint him; for this is the one" (1 Sam. 16:12).

Something astounding happened in David's life when Samuel anointed him. Scripture says, "the Spirit of the Lord came upon David from that day forward" (1 Sam. 16:13). David knew that something had changed in his life. Many commentators believe that at this time Samuel told David that he would be the next king of Israel.[28] However, before that would come to pass, he would have to go back to tending sheep.

Carnival Beat Down

Growing up, I had a hard time keeping my mouth shut. I was normally shy in public, but when I was with friends I would rattle my mouth. On one particular occasion, I said a little too much, and it cost me. My best friend and I wanted to go to the carnival at the Winn-Dixie parking lot. We were young, and there was a lot of excitement surrounding the carnival. My mom took us, and she stayed in the parking lot while we enjoyed the rides.

Everything was going well until we got on the Ferris wheel. As the Ferris wheel went up, we noticed that some moisture was coming down on us. I looked up and saw a longhaired redneck spitting on us. We didn't pay for that. He was ruining our ride, and somebody needed to say something. However, this guy was big, and I was a late-blooming thirteen-year-old. He probably had me by four years and eighty pounds.

In spite of the mismatch, I could not keep quiet. So, I told him to stop spitting on us and he laughed at me. All the while, my friend was begging me to keep quiet, but it was too late. Before I knew what was happening I said something I wished I could take back. In a loud voice I said, "Is that a boy or a girl in front of us?"

---

[28] Warren Wiersbe, *Be Successful* (Colorado Springs, CO: David C. Cook, 2001), 104.

I cannot emphasize enough what a bad move that was. The longhaired redneck turned and pointed at me and said he was going to get me when we got off of the ride. I was scared.

Fortunately, when the ride stopped, I was able to join an older crowd of boys who were at the carnival with my big brother. I thought the situation was over; however, one of the axioms of life is that when you call a boy almost twice your size a girl, the situation is not over until the bigger boy says it is over.

A few minutes later as I was walking by the concession stand, two big hands suddenly grabbed me and pulled me behind the trailer. We were out of sight. It was only me, my friend, the longhaired redneck, and his friend. He lifted me off the ground and told me to give him money for a ticket. I refused, and he slapped me upside the head. Once again, he told me to give him some money. Stubbornly, I said no and promptly received another pop to the head.

As I was getting roughed up, I saw my momma sitting in her car with a clear line of sight to what was going on. I kept hoping she would see the grave situation I had put myself in. All I needed was for her to see what was happening to her boy. Finally, she made eye contact with the beat down. As she exited the car and made her way toward us, I told the guy I would give him the money. As soon as he let me down, my momma was all over him. She verbally destroyed him. She saved me from the bully.

David was also going to have an encounter with a bully. This guy was huge. He was not some longhaired redneck looking for ticket money. He was a nine-foot-tall, battle-hardened Philistine looking for a head to mount on his spear.

Too Big to Miss

As is often the case, a seminal event catapulted David from the ordinary to the extraordinary. The Israelites were at war with their long-time nemesis, the Philistines. The two armies were arrayed in battle on both sides of a valley. Every day a big guy from the Philistine army named Goliath went down into the valley and challenged the army of Israel to send a soldier down to fight him. Understandably, none of Saul's men wanted to fight a giant who stood over nine feet tall, whose body was encased in metal armor, and who had a spear with a head on it that weighed over fifteen pounds.[29]

King Saul tried to incentivize his troops so someone would step forward and fight Goliath. He promised great rewards to anyone who could defeat Goliath. These rewards included marriage to his daughter and a substantial tax cut (1 Sam. 17:25). However, no one would take Saul up on his offer because Goliath seemed unbeatable. Twice daily for forty days Goliath issued his challenge, and no one responded. Everyone was afraid. But everything changed when David arrived.

David's seven older brothers were in the army serving King Saul, and Jesse had sent him to the camp with bread and cheese for his brothers and their commanders. When David arrived, he heard Goliath deriding Israel and its God, and he wanted to do something about it. David approached King Saul and said, "Let

---

[29] Robert D. Bergen, *The New American Commentary*: 1, 2 Samuel, Vol. 7 (Nashville, TN: Broadman and Holman, 1996), 189–90.

no man's heart fail because of him; your servant will go and fight with this Philistine" (1 Sam. 17:32).

At this point, David had already been discouraged by one of his brothers and subsequently by King Saul from taking up the fight. But David had a track record of doing the impossible. With God's strength, he had killed a bear and a lion during his days as a shepherd, and David saw this Philistine as more of the same. As far as David was concerned, Goliath's defiance of the armies of the living God had to be stopped.

When King Saul saw how determined David was to fight Goliath, he gave his consent and offered David his armor. Because the gear was so bulky and heavy, David refused to wear it. So, he went into the valley alone with only a slingshot and five stones. Although a mere teenager, David had God on his side.

When Goliath saw David, he was insulted that David was the best that the Israelites could muster. As David closed in on Goliath, the giant told David all of the bad stuff that he was going to do to him. David's response was classic. He revealed the source of his courage and answered Goliath's taunts:

> You come to me with a sword, with a spear, and with a javelin. But I come to you in the name of the Lord of hosts, the God of the armies of Israel, whom you have defied. This day the Lord will deliver you into my hand, and I will strike you and take your head from you. And this day I will give the carcasses of the camp of the Philistines to the birds of the air and the wild beasts of the

earth, that all the earth may know that there is a
God in Israel. (1 Sam. 17:45–46)

Without warning, David whirled his slingshot and sent
a rock crashing into Goliath's forehead. Before the fallen
giant could regain consciousness, David used Goliath's own
sword and cut off his head. Upon this decapitation of their
foe's champion, the army of Israel rallied behind David and
attacked the Philistines to win the battle. David's life was
forever changed by this feat.

Wonder Boy or One-Hit Wonder

The entertainment world is full of one-hit wonders. As a
matter of fact, September 25 is National One-Hit Wonder Day.
This day recognizes the musical artists who cracked the Top
40 only once, such as Tiny Tim with "Tip-Toe through the
Tulips" and Taco with "Putting on the Ritz."[30] Another song
that warrants the one-hit wonder label is "Who Let the Dogs
Out?" by the Baha Men.[31]

These examples serve as reminders that just because you
succeed once in life, it doesn't mean that you will enjoy similar
success again. A one-hit wonder is left with a lot of life to

---

[30] "National One-Hit Wonder Day—September 25," National Day Calendar,
www.nationaldaycalendar.com/national-one-hit-wonder-day-september-25/.
[31] Ariana Bacle, Eric Brown, Dana Rose Falcone, and Christian Holub, "What
Comes After the One-Hit Wonder?" *Entertainment Weekly*, September 25, 2015.
www.ew.com/article/2015/09/25/national-one-hit-wonder-day-second-single.

live. Fortunately, David would not become the original one-hit wonder, experiencing instead an unrivaled string of early successes.

Moving on Up

During the next few years, David became King Saul's finest general. He was such a good military commander that the young women would dance around him singing, "Saul has slain his thousands, and David his ten thousands" (1 Sam. 18:7). As could be predicted, Saul viewed David's ascendency as a direct threat to his kingdom.

A sinister disposition began to overtake Saul, but David behaved wisely, and the Lord was with him. David's impeccable behavior and demeanor made Saul even more afraid of him, while the people grew to love him even more. He was a man on the rise. He was even engaged to marry Saul's oldest daughter.

When the time arrived for the marriage, however, Saul callously gave his promised daughter to another man, though he agreed to let David wed his youngest daughter, Michal. Through back channels, Saul let David know that the unofficial dowry for Michal's hand in marriage was one hundred Philistine foreskins, hoping that David would die while attempting to meet that expectation.

David accepted the challenge, and as a sign of his zeal to be part of the king's family, he killed two hundred Philistines and cut off their foreskins. David presented these phallic remnants to Saul as payment for his daughter.

With the dowry paid, David was allowed to marry Michal. His behavior only gave Saul more confirmation that David was blessed by God. This increased awareness of God's favor made Saul even more jealous and committed to David's demise.

You Too, Brutus

It's funny how life can change. When I was called to the church I left, there was a standing ovation when the vote tally was announced. People were excited. I was excited. I even made the front page of the local newspaper.

It was great until the conflicts started. There was so much to overcome. There was systemic dysfunctionality throughout the church. Problems that should have been addressed years earlier had been neglected, and now they were being presented to me all at once. It was a case of good people in a bad system. The system of church polity was rigged to fail. I was even told later by a denominational leader who had intimate knowledge of the church that he knew that the next pastor of the church would fail. I wish he had been that candid with me before I came. Oh well, water under the bridge.

During the midst of one of the most intense intramural church skirmishes, there was a particular man who I considered a friend who asked to meet with me after church one night. I remember when he came into my office. I felt like I could relax with this guy because he was a good friend. I must admit I did not see what was coming. He let me have it.

It's safe to say it was one of the top five worst experiences I have had in the ministry. He told me he even doubted that God had ever called me to the ministry. I was devastated. He was supposed to be my friend. I had let my guard down, and he gave me a left hook. When he was through all I could ask was, "Will you pray for me?"

When I got home, my wife was still at choir practice, so I went and laid down on one of my girl's beds. My oldest daughter sat beside me as I laid on my stomach with my face in my hands. My youngest daughter picked up her Bible and started reading scripture to me. She just randomly read Psalm 17, and I couldn't believe what I was hearing. It was just what I needed. Here's what it says:

> Hear a just cause, O Lord, Attend to my cry; Give ear to my prayer which is not from deceitful lips. Let my vindication come from your presence; Let Your eyes look on the things that are upright. You have tested my heart; You have visited me in the night; You have tried me and have found nothing; I have purposed that my mouth shall not transgress. Concerning the works of men, By the word of Your lips, I have kept away from the paths of the destroyer. Uphold my steps in your paths, That my footsteps may not slip. (Psalm 17:1–5).

Wow! It was just what I needed. These words of scripture medicated my soul and gave me hope as I faced an increasingly hostile situation.

Man on the Run

As time progressed, Saul began to plot a way to kill David. He told his son, Jonathan, and his other leaders that he wanted David put to death. Fortunately, Jonathan was able to talk Saul out of his plans, but Saul's madness continued.

While Saul was dealing with spiritual oppression, he called for David, the mighty warrior, to play music for him to ease his spirit. While David played, Saul attempted to pin him to the wall with a spear. David narrowly escaped and went to his chambers to be with his wife, who advised him to flee immediately.

After early success in life, David began his later years on the run. The precariousness of his situation is revealed through his own words: "there is but a step between me and death" (1 Sam. 20:3). What do you do when there is only a step between you and death? You keep running. You run as fast and as far as you can to find a safe haven.

For David, this journey ironically led him to the land of Israel's enemy. In an incredible lapse of judgment, David sought refuge in the land of the Philistines. Unfortunately, the Philistines recognized David as the one who had killed many of their soldiers in battle, and they took him into custody. David pretended to be a madman by scratching on doors like an animal and letting saliva run down his beard in order to escape. Assuming that he was insane, the Philistines let him go.

David had suffered a severe reversal of fortune. He had gone from being the good-looking military hero married to the king's daughter to a man on the run, pretending to be crazy. Fear had so clouded his thinking that a decision to seek refuge with the Philistines had almost cost him his life. While reflecting upon his near escape, David wrote, "God is for me" (Psalm 56:9).

Think about that statement. At the time King Saul was using all of his resources to kill David; the Philistines had almost put him to death; all types of lies were being spoken about him. It seemed as though no one was on his side, yet David knew that God was for him, and that was enough to sustain him.

What Happened to God's Favor?

During some of my darkest days, I had to remind myself that God is for me. I was finding it hard to put all of the pieces together and still feel like I had God's favor.

One day in particular stands out. I was desperate to know that I had God's favor on my life. Even though I had times where I thought God was against me, I knew theologically that He was for me. Romans 8:31 says, "If God is for us, who can be against us?" However, I needed something more. I needed to see it. I needed to hear it.

As I grabbed a few items from the local Kroger, I was desperately praying that God would show me a sign of His favor. I just really needed something. When I went to check out, the cashier and I got into a conversation about her walk with Christ. She said that she wanted to show me the prayer that she prays every day. When I read it, I was blown away. It said, "This is going to be a great day. God is guiding and directing my steps.

His favor is surrounding me. Goodness and mercy are following me. I am excited about today."

When I read, "His favor is surrounding me," I couldn't believe it. I had just prayed less than five minutes earlier that God would show me a sign of His favor, and then the cashier showed me a prayer about having God's favor. Coincidence? I think not.

No Good Deed Goes Unpunished

After David fled from the Philistines, he wound up in a No Man's Land where he took refuge in the caves of Adullam. While he was there, his family joined him, as well as those who were in distress, in debt, or bitter of soul (1 Sam. 22:2). The misfits found refuge with David. In the early days, the number of fighting men who had joined him numbered four hundred.

David began an eight-year odyssey of running for his life. Over and over again he had to take it on the chin even though he had plenty of opportunities to ruin his testimony by acts of desperation or revenge. Once, when a Jewish city named Keilah was under attack by the Philistines, David and his men risked their lives to deliver it. As a show of their appreciation, the people of the city decided to turn him over to King Saul (1 Sam. 23:1–14). Fortunately, David and his men were able to escape before Saul's forces arrived.

Additionally, David spared King Saul's life twice, once while he was using the bathroom in a cave and another time while he was sleeping. David knew that it was not his place to take the life of the king. He said to his men, "Do not destroy him; for who can stretch out his hand against the Lord's anointed, and be guiltless? As the Lord lives, the Lord shall strike him, or his day shall come to die, or he shall go out to battle and perish. The Lord forbid that I should stretch out my hand against the Lord's anointed" (1 Sam. 26:9–11). David knew that he would not become king until Saul died but that Saul's life was in God's hands.

It's Hard Trying to Survive

There was a period of time when I didn't know if we were going to make it financially at the new church I started, so I had to try to supplement my income. A friend of mine had a job doing housing inspections on foreclosed homes. It was pretty simple. Drive to the property, see if the power and water were cut off, assess any damages, and send in the report. How hard could that be? Well, that was not the question. The question should have been, how dangerous could that be? My route took me to some of the most dangerous neighborhoods in Atlanta. I read where one of the neighborhoods had been listed as one of the top ten most dangerous in the United States.

One day while I was inspecting homes in a neighborhood near the federal penitentiary in Atlanta, I got a little careless and lost awareness of my surroundings. As I was confirming the vacancy of a residence, I suddenly noticed there was a man standing between my car and me. It was pretty evident that he was up to no good, and I was not a neighborhood regular. I looked around, and the street was empty. It was just me and him.

As I tried to decide what to do, a truck suddenly appeared. When the man saw the truck, he immediately took off running. Whatever he had in mind was foiled by the sudden appearance of that truck. Needless to say, the whole episode shook me up a little. All I could think is, *What am I doing? This isn't what I signed up to do.* But it didn't matter. When you are in the wilderness, there are times when survival takes precedence over vision. You do what you have to do to make it as long as you don't violate scripture.

No Respect

During the time of David's banishment, the prophet Samuel died. Remember, Samuel was the one who had anointed David to be the next king of Israel. The only one who could vouch for David having been chosen by God to be king was dead.

Also during this time, a wealthy man named Nabal disrespected David. He so infuriated David by ill treatment of his men that David responded by mustering his troops to kill all the males in Nabal's household. However, Nabal's wife, Abigail, intercepted David before he arrived and talked him out of it. She acknowledged that God had incredible plans for David and that he should not do anything that could later be used against him. She said:

> And it shall come to pass, when the Lord has done for my lord according to all the good He has spoken concerning you, and has appointed you ruler over Israel, that this will be no grief

to you, nor offense of heart to my lord, either that you have shed blood without cause, or that my lord has avenged himself. But when the Lord has dealt well with my lord then remember your maidservant. (1 Sam. 25:30–31)

With her wise words, Abigail helped David stay focused on the big picture of God's plan. She looked out for him when his judgment was too clouded for him to look out for himself.

Let Him Eat Cake

Several years into my wilderness experience, I felt like I had come to a dead end. The church had plateaued and was starting to ebb in attendance. My passion was waning, and I felt the constant pressure of just getting by. Consequently, I started thinking that the church might do better under different leadership. So, we contacted a large church in our area and began to discuss the possibility of becoming their satellite location. At the time, we met in the movie theater at the local mall, and our site would serve the larger church well in their pursuit to expand.

I must admit that this was one of the most humbling times of my life. The other church was very interested, but their conditions came across more as a takeover than a partnership. They would assume all of our assets and location, and our two part-time staff members and myself would be released. In other words, we would be fired. It wasn't exactly what I was expecting, but I was so low that I was willing to go with it.

Our leadership team met with theirs at a local Italian restaurant to discuss the deal. I remember sitting there and keeping my head down while I ate a big piece of chocolate cake. The two groups discussed the takeover. It was said that whatever severance package I received would be the responsibility of our church. Once the merger happened, I was on my own. As I said, I would have gone along with this agreement. Fortunately, my wife and one of our key leaders were adamantly opposed to the deal. They thought it was not fair, and they were looking out for me when I was too low to look out for myself.

We made an offer that we knew the other church would refuse, and they did. Looking back, I am so glad that others stepped in and looked out for me when I was too worn out to do it myself. I needed others. I couldn't make it on my own.

CHAPTER 4

Staying Focused

The ability to maintain focus cannot be overestimated, especially during times of crisis. Often, when someone in the military or law enforcement performs an incredible act of heroism, he says that his training took over. These individuals know how to act in unexpected situations because they have been taught to stay focused.

To a lesser degree, some television personalities are also taught how to stay on task when the unexpected happens. Take, for instance, Jim Cantorre of the Weather Channel. He made national news and became a YouTube sensation when he covered a winter storm in Charleston, South Carolina.[32] During his live broadcast, a loud voice was heard before a young man suddenly appeared running toward Cantorre. As he reached to grab the weatherman, Cantorre kneed the young man in

---

[32] Philip Weiss, "C of C Student Who Had Run-in with Cantorre Says He Would Do It Again," Live 5 News, January 30, 2014. http://www.live5news.com/story/24567796/weather-channels-jim-cantore-rushed-by-kid-delivers-knee.

the midsection and continued talking as though nothing had happened. Cantorre didn't miss a beat. Like Cantorre, we must stay focused on God's purpose for our lives even when it seems like all is lost.

When All Seems Lost

Toward the end of his time in the wilderness, David was presented with an unexpected situation that required intense focus. Although his present situation was riddled with trouble, he had to keep in mind that his future held promise. He was to be the next king of Israel. Circumstantially, everything made that prospect look unlikely. David was a fugitive, and many had lost respect for him. Then another crisis arose.

David and his men had made an uneasy alliance with their enemies, the Philistines. When the Philistines were preparing for battle, David and his men showed up to assist them. However, the Philistines refused to let them fight, so David and his men returned to their families, who were living in Ziklag.

Before they returned home, the Amalekites invaded Ziklag, burned the city, and took David and his men's wives and children as captives. When David and his men arrived home and saw what had happened, they were so distraught that they wept, "until they had no more power to weep" (1 Sam. 30:4). In their despondency, David's army directed their anger toward him. Their pain was so intense that they wanted to stone David.

In the midst of his own pain, David had to keep his cool. Not only had he lost his family to the Amalekites, but now his own trusted men wanted to kill him. He had to act quickly and with wisdom.

This had to be the lowest of lows for David. His family had been abducted, and his men wanted to kill him. However, he did something interesting. Scripture says, "But David strengthened himself in the Lord his God" (1 Sam. 30:6). He had nowhere else to turn. Things were as dark as they could get.

Boxing great Mike Tyson once said, "Everyone has a plan till' they get punched in the mouth."[33] David had just gotten punched in the mouth and kicked in the groin, but he did not give up. He strengthened himself in the Lord. He had to do for himself what no one else could do for him. This was the key moment in his life. There was no room for error; he could not falter. Too much was at stake. He had to remember God's word, and he had to dig deep.

Scripture tells us that David remained calm and called for the priest. David consulted God and asked for guidance. God's instructions were very clear. David obeyed and led his men in pursuit of the Amalekites, and he delivered all who had been taken captive. Instead of folding like a house of cards, he strengthened himself in the Lord, avoided disaster, and lived to fight another day.

At the same time, unbeknownst to David, Saul and three of his sons were involved in the battle that would end their lives. As the army of Israel fought it out with the Philistines on Mount Gilboa, Saul and his sons were tragically killed. The obstacle standing in the way of David becoming king had just been removed. All David knew, though, was that he had just

---

[33] http://www.brainyquote.com/quotes/authors/m/mike_tyson.html.

avoided a deadly rebellion by his own men. He was still just trying to survive.

When word of Saul's demise reached David, he asked God what he should do next and was told to go to Hebron in Judah, where he would be anointed as king. So, at the young age of thirty, David became king over Judah (2 Sam. 5:4). It took another seven years of demonstrating strength before he became king over all of Israel.

Samuel's words to a young shepherd boy had finally come to pass. The shepherd boy, David, had become king of Israel. His reign would be like none other because from his lineage would come the King of Kings, Jesus Christ.

Putting It All Together

Before he became king, David experienced incredible ups and downs. He went from being the heartthrob of the nation to a refugee barely able to stay alive. However, he had a solid base on which he lived his life. He was grounded in his faith in a God he could not see. God was so real to David that he poured out his heart to Him in the Psalms.

During one of his darkest days, David recorded these words in Psalm 56:9: "This I know, because God is for me." David knew that God was for him in spite of what his circumstances were screaming at him. Romans 8:31 reminds us, "If God is for us, who can be against us?"

Have your circumstances led you to think that God is against you? Do you truly believe that God is for you?

During David's eight years in the wilderness while running

from Saul, he didn't have much time or motivation to plan for the future. As a matter of fact, his goal was just to stay alive. To believe what had been spoken to him as a boy by the prophet Samuel probably seemed like fanciful words at times. However, David found it within himself to hold on to the belief that he would someday be king.

On one occasion when he was hiding in a cave while King Saul pursued him, David wrote these words of assurance: "I will cry out to God Most High, to God who performs all things for me" (Psalm 57:2). He still found it within himself to believe that God would fulfill His purpose in his life even when it looked as though it would never happen.

David didn't give up on his faith. He persevered and eventually prevailed. Galatians 6:9 says, "And let us not grow weary while doing good, for in due season we shall reap if we do not lose heart." Don't give up.

David almost threw caution to the wind when he went to kill Nabal. He temporarily lost sight of the prize. Fortunately, Abigail was there to remind him of his purpose.

Have you thought about giving up on your faith? Do you have faith that you will reap what God has for you if you don't give up? If you do give up, what effect will that have on the lives of others?

Perhaps the most crucial time in David's wilderness experience was at the very end when the Amalekites kidnapped everyone's wives and children and his men wanted to kill him. Although he had no family or trusted men left, he strengthened himself in the Lord. When everyone else had turned on him, David went to the Lord for wisdom, and the Lord delivered.

Are you at a point in life where it seems as though others have lost their confidence in you? Do you know how to strengthen yourself in the Lord?

David could not control his own future. He could not become king until Saul died. On two occasions David could have killed Saul, but he didn't. He knew that Saul's life was in the hands of God and that when God was ready for Saul to die, it would happen. David had to resist the temptation to make things happen himself. He had to be content for his life to unfold according to God's timetable and not his own.

Have you gotten out of God's will by trying to make things happen before it is time?

Look Out for Depression

When we are forced to wait on the intervention of God in our lives, it is easy to give into depression. Oftentimes that feeling of despair makes us feel helpless. If left unattended, helplessness translates into hopelessness, and that is not good. Wrong thought patterns could wreck your state of mind. Read Psalms 42 and 43 and see how the Psalmist alternates between thoughts of hope and depression. He goes up and then he goes back down. However, from these psalms we can identify three shortcuts to depression that we all too often find ourselves on.

The first shortcut to depression comes when we feel cut off from purpose. The writer of the psalm was a son of Korah. He had the responsibility of providing music at the temple. His problem was that he was no longer in Jerusalem but was in a forced exile cut off from his God-ordained role at the temple. His sense of purpose had vanished.

The solution to this temptation toward depression is to serve God where you are with all you have. God still has a purpose for your life. Ecclesiastes 9:10 says, "Whatever your hand finds to do, do it with your might; for there is no work or device or knowledge or wisdom in the grave where you are going." In other words, whatever you are doing, give it all you have because when you die, this opportunity comes to a close.

In the New Testament, the apostle Paul writes in Colossians 3:17, "And whatever you do in word or deed, do all in the name of the Lord Jesus, giving thanks to God the Father through Him." As long as you are alive, you have the purpose of serving God through whatever you are doing. This purpose lasts all your life. The particulars may change, but the goal remains the same, so get busy and get yourself out of that pit.

The second shortcut to depression is what we will call demoralizing nostalgia. This depression sets in when the memories in our minds cross the line from inspiring us in the present to burying us in the past. Our fixation with a romanticized past makes our present situation even more unbearable.

We need to realize that the past is history. We cannot go back. When we allow ourselves to be defeated in the present by nostalgia from the past, we have ceased to live as God intended us to live. If we need to get nostalgic, then we need to get nostalgic about our relationship with Christ and how it was when we first stepped across that threshold of faith.

In Revelation 2, Jesus addresses the church at Ephesus. He

chastises them for leaving their first love. He encourages them to think back to how it was when they first believed. He desires them to get back to that point. He says, "Nevertheless I have this against you, that you have left your first love. Remember therefore from where you have fallen; repent and do the first works" (Rev. 2:4–5). He wanted them to remember how it was when they first believed and let that memory inspire their lives in the present.

So, if you need to get nostalgic, then get nostalgic about when you walked closest with Christ. Allow those memories to inspire you in the present to get back to where you need to be spiritually.

The final shortcut to depression that we find in this passage is perhaps the hardest one to deal with. This shortcut happens when we live life with a lack of circumstantial awareness of the presence of God. When it seems like we have lost the favor of God and prayers are no longer being answered.

The psalmist asks such questions as, "Why have You forgotten me?" (Psalm 42:9) and "Why do you cast me off?" (Psalm 43:2). He feels forgotten by God. Meanwhile, his enemies continue to ask where his God is. The only voices he is hearing now are the ones who question God's involvement in his life. There is no encouragement. There is no circumstantial evidence of God's activity on his behalf, and he cannot understand why. He struggles with hopelessness and despair.

The solution to this is to put your hope in God. Walk by faith. Hebrews 11:1 and 6 says, "Now faith is the substance of things hoped for, the evidence of things not seen ... But without faith it is impossible to please Him, for he who comes to God must believe that He is, and that He is a rewarder of those who diligently seek Him." These verses make it adamantly clear that we must walk by faith and believe that God rewards those that diligently seek Him.

Faith does make a difference. God does bless those who walk by faith. He says so in His word. He decides how the blessing will come, but He will bless. Our responsibility is to not give up. Giving up can cause one to miss the blessing of God. Galatians 6:9 says, "And let us not grow weary while doing good, for in due season we shall reap if we do not lose heart."

It is to our advantage not to give up. Trust God, and see things through. He has not forsaken you. He loves you. He is for you. He is a rewarder of those who diligently seek Him. Just like the psalmist, we need to talk to ourselves. We need to tell ourselves to get out of the pit and hope in God.

PART III

Saul

Success after a Midlife Change

CHAPTER 5

Accepting God's Call

Many casual readers of scripture assume that when Saul was converted on the road to Damascus, his life immediately improved. Others think that he immediately began his career as a missionary and writer of scripture. Nothing could be further from the truth.

Part of the reason for this misconception is that the flow of time is condensed in the book of Acts. When Saul was converted, he was told that he would proclaim the gospel before Gentiles, kings, and the children of Israel. However, as we will see, it took years before this happened.

A Warlord Makes Peace

Saul's conversion is perhaps the most famous in all of Christian history. His coming to faith is referred to as the "Damascus Road experience." We even use this phrase today when someone has a profound change of heart.

Perhaps no one else in recent history has experienced such a radical transformation as Joshua Milton Blahyi, also known as General Butt Naked. Blahyi was the most feared warlord during Liberia's civil war in the 1990s. He originally came to power as a spiritual advisor to President Samuel Doe. However, the spiritual connection he had was with darkness.

During battle, Blahyi wore only a pair of shoes, believing that his nakedness made him an invisible target for bullets. As a sacrifice to Satan before his battles, he would kill a child and eat his or her heart. His morbid obsession with darkness and death made him the most feared man in Liberia. By his own admission, he was responsible for the deaths of twenty thousand Liberians.[34] If there ever was a despicable human being, it was Blahyi. During one of his battles, something incredible happened to him. This is how *The New Yorker* magazine recounts his life-changing experience:

> In his memoir Blahyi describes killing a child near [a] bridge by "opening the little girl's back and plucking out her heart." Her blood was still on his hands, he told me, when he heard a voice. "When I looked back, I saw a man standing there. He was so bright, brighter than the sun."

---

[34] Eryn Sun, "African Warlord Who Killed 20,000 People Repents: Now Christian Evangelist," *The Christian Post*, December 23, 2011. http://www.christianpost.com/news/african-warlord-who-killed-20000-people-repents-now-christian-evangelist-65550/.

The voice told him, "Repent and live, or refuse and die."[35]

Blahyi believed the voice to be that of Jesus. In the midst of battle and while committing an atrocity beyond imagination, Blahyi claimed that an encounter with Jesus forever changed his life.

In the foreword to Blahyi's biography, *The Redemption of an African Warlord,* Pastor Bojan Jancic writes, "Not since the conversion of Saul of Tarsus on the Road to Damascus have I heard a conversion story more radically compelling than that of former African warlord, General Butt Naked."[36]

Blahyi's amazing story is a Damascus Road experience. Now let's return to where the phrase started—with a man on a mission to rid the world of the name of Jesus.

Promise

The first introduction of Saul of Tarsus is in Acts 7 at the stoning of Stephen, the first Christian martyr. As the mob descended upon Stephen to stone him to death because of his faith in Jesus, scripture says, "And the witnesses laid down their clothes at the feet of a young man named Saul" (Acts 7:58).

Some believe that Saul had some type of authority over

---

[35] Damon Tabor, "The Greater the Sinner: A Liberian Warlord's Unlikely Path to Forgiveness," *The New Yorker,* March 14, 2016. http://www.newyorker.com/magazine/2016/03/14/general-butt-naked-the-repentant-warlord.

[36] Joshua Blahyi, *The Redemption of an African Warlord* (Shippensburg, PA: Destiny Image Publishers, 2013), 17.

what happened to Stephen. His official title at this time is not known, but his approval served to intensify the violent reaction to Stephen's witness.[37] As a matter of fact, it seems that Stephen's death incited something deep within Saul.

After Stephen died, scripture tells us that an intense persecution was launched against the church at Jerusalem and that Saul was the main instigator. Saul "made havoc of the church, entering every house, and dragging off men and women, committing them to prison" (Acts 8:3). In Greek literature, the phrase "made havoc" is used to describe how a wild beast tears open its prey.[38] Saul savagely attacked the church like a wild animal. His intensity was otherworldly. He intentionally separated husbands and wives from one another and consented to the deaths of Christians.

Saul is not mentioned again until the next chapter in Acts, where he is reintroduced. "Then Saul, still breathing threats and murder against the disciples of the Lord" (Acts 9:1). Saul's desire to wipe out the church was an obsession. Famed biblical scholar A. T. Robertson describes Saul's state of mind by observing, "The taste of blood in the death of Stephen was pleasing to young Saul, and now he reveled in the slaughter of the saints both men and women."[39]

Saul was single-minded in his mania to obliterate the name of Jesus. Years later he recounted his state of mind before his

[37] Kenneth O. Gangel and Holmon, *New Testament Commentary: Acts*, Vol. 5 (Nashville, TN: Broadman and Holman, 1998), 111.

[38] John MacArthur, *The MacArthur New Testament Commentary: Acts 1–12* (Chicago, IL: Moody Press, 1994), 231.

[39] A. T. Robertson, *Word Pictures in the New Testament*: Vol. 3 (Grand Rapids, MI: Baker Books, 1930), 113.

conversion. "I persecuted the church of God beyond measure and tried to destroy it" (Gal. 1:13).

Don't Let Hate Motivate

Hate is a powerful motivator. It is so strong that it can easily become one's master. History is replete with people who allowed hatred to dominate their lives. Take, for instance, the Marxist leader Che Guevara, who is famous for saying, "A revolutionary must become a cold killing machine motivated by pure hate."[40] Guevara's hatred was an indispensable part of his revolutionary ideology. It led to countless deaths and eventually set the stage for his capture and execution.

Motivated by pure hatred, Saul asked the Jewish leaders for special permission to go to Damascus for the purpose of arresting Jewish followers of Jesus and extraditing them back to Jerusalem for punishment. His request was within the bounds of the law. The Romans had granted the Jewish high priest the authority to exercise control over Jewish communities throughout the empire.[41] Saul's mission would be carried out with a religious zeal that was reinforced by Roman law.

As Saul began the 135-mile journey to Damascus, one can only imagine the hatred that coursed through his veins. However, an unseen battle raged within him. Saul was a man fighting the conviction that Jesus Christ was the Son of God. Scripture makes

---

[40] http://www.azquotes.com/quote/716640.

[41] Mal Couch and Ed Hindson, *Acts: Witness to the World* (Chattanooga, TN: AMG Publishers, 2004), 133.

us aware of this internal struggle when Saul was on the outskirts of Damascus.

Intercepted by Christ

I was a huge Atlanta Falcons fan as a boy. Back in the 1970s, the Falcons were just plain terrible. Former Atlanta running back Dave Hampton perfectly illustrated their futility. During the last game of the 1972 season, he became the first player in Falcons history to rush for a thousand yards. There was a brief celebration to commemorate this historic event, but unfortunately, he was stopped for a six-yard loss on the next play and didn't get another carry. Consequently, he finished the year with 995 yards.[42] His luck seemed to epitomize the Falcons during those early years. However, in 1975 the team drafted Steve Bartkowski, the number-one pick in the NFL draft. It took a few years, but he eventually led the Falcons to the playoffs. He became one of the most popular sports personalities in the history of Atlanta.

Perhaps my favorite memory of Bartkowski is the book written about his conversion to Christ. Titled *Intercepted by Christ*, it captures the life-altering transformation that Christ brought into his life. When a quarterback's throw is intercepted, the ball goes in the exact opposite direction. What a wonderful way to look at a life that is changed by Christ.

Bartkowski lists the following changes as evidence that Christ intercepted his life: "First, there was peace and freedom

---

[42] "1,000 Yards That Wasn't," *Atlanta Journal and Constitution*, 1972, http://ajc.com/photo/sports/1000-yards-wasn't/pCw2FY/

from pressure for the first time ever. Second, there was a hunger for the Word. Third, there was a confidence and security that God was in control of events. Fourthly, my lifestyle changed dramatically."[43] That's what happened to Steve Bartkowski when Christ dramatically transformed him. Now let's look at how Saul's life changed when the risen Lord Jesus Christ stopped him in his tracks.

The Original Damascus Road Experience

As Saul made his way to Damascus, he was suddenly brought to his knees by a bright light. When he tried to gather himself, a voice spoke to him from within the light and said, "Saul, Saul, why are you persecuting Me?" (Acts 9:4). It was none other than the Lord Jesus Christ speaking to him directly from heaven.

A stunned Saul uttered, "Who are you, Lord?" The voice replied, "I am Jesus, whom you are persecuting." With these words Jesus let Saul know that the persecutions he had been carrying out were personal. Saul was humbled and physically blinded by the encounter. At this point, Saul was willing to accept the terms of surrender. He then was directed to go into Damascus and await further instruction. Having been blinded by the light, Saul was led into the city by his companions.

Scripture tells us that God spoke to one of the prominent believers in Damascus, a man named Ananias, and told him to go to where Saul was staying and lay hands on him so that he might

---

[43] Dan DeHaan, *Intercepted by Christ* (Lilburn, GA: Cross Roads Books), 42.

regain his sight. The directive stunned Ananias. He had heard that Saul was in town to arrest Christians and send them bound back to Jerusalem. He had no idea of what God had done in Saul's life. However, the Lord told Ananias enough to encourage him to go on his mission.

In a vision, Jesus revealed to Ananias that Saul was a "chosen vessel of Mine to bear My name before Gentiles, kings, and the children of Israel. For I will show him how many things he must suffer for My Name's sake" (Acts 9:15–16).

After hearing these words, Ananias went to Saul, laid his hands on him, and said, "Brother Saul, the Lord Jesus, who appeared to you on the road as you came, has sent me that you may receive your sight and be filled with the Holy Spirit" (Acts 9:17). At this proclamation, the scales fell off Saul's eyes, and he was filled with the Holy Spirit. He was then baptized as an outward identification of his newfound faith in Jesus.

Saul was utterly changed. His friends became his enemies, and those he once persecuted became his friends. His world was turned upside down, or as some would say, right-side up.

Can Somebody Help a Brother Out?

After astonishing Damascus with the testimony of his newfound faith, Saul spent the next three years in the Arabian Desert poring over the Old Testament and growing in his walk with Christ. When he reappeared in Damascus, his testimony was so strong that the Jews plotted to kill him. In order to preserve his life, his fellow believers lowered him over the city wall in a basket so he could make his way to Jerusalem.

Once in Jerusalem, Saul tried to join the church, but everyone was still terrified of him. A trusted believer named Barnabas vouched for Saul and his sincerity, and once Saul was accepted into the church, he shared the gospel all over Jerusalem. However, according to Galatians 1:18, his stay in Jerusalem lasted only fifteen days. The power of his witness was the cause of his short stay. The Jews could not match the wisdom and power of his words, so once again a plot was hatched to kill Saul.

When the church found out about this plan, they sent Saul away for his safety to his home region of Cilicia, where Tarsus is located. Saul spent some prime years of his life toiling away in Cilicia under the radar. There was no fanfare, no headlines. Just years spent faithfully laboring away for the kingdom.

New Opportunity Brings More Critics

During my wilderness experience, I tried to lay low. It took me a while to get over all the shots I had taken. Five years into my ordeal, I was presented with a most unusual opportunity. The state television network in Finland, YLE, asked if I would be willing to come to Northern Europe for a week and serve as a representative for American Evangelicals. They were doing a documentary called *The Norden*. My role would be to compare and contrast how Americans and Scandinavians approach faith. As you can imagine, my wife and I thoroughly checked out the credibility of the ones asking for my participation, and surprisingly everything turned out to be legit.

In December of 2012, I left the United States for the first time and went to northern Europe all by myself. Having been given a brief itinerary, I decided that all my answers would be very straightforward. Nothing would be nuanced. You see, Scandinavia is perhaps the most secular region on the face of the earth. As such, I felt like Christians in these nations needed some validation. They needed to know that someone still held to biblical values.

I did my homework before I left, and I knew the direction I wanted to take the conversations. This was no time to be faint of heart. I was given an incredible opportunity to speak truth to a part of the world that had supposedly gotten over the concept of God.

I arrived in Denmark on a snowy December afternoon. Over the next week, I was filmed challenging a couple of liberal state church priests in Denmark on the topic of same-sex marriage. I debated the subject of evolution with a secular humanist in Sweden, and I attended a heavy metal mass in Finland. It was an incredible week. The camera crew from YLE was very good to me.

The series aired on state television in Finland, Denmark, and Sweden in November 2014 and also became a YouTube sensation. It was nominated for some awards; however, I was not prepared for the backlash it would create.

Atheists from all over the world attacked me. A clip of the documentary became the most viewed video on a popular atheist website. An atheist talk show host made me the subject of one of his broadcasts. I received all kinds of nasty emails. I was called almost every name in the book. Why? Because I dared cast doubt on the theory of evolution, and I did not agree with same-sex marriage.

I wish I could say that the criticism didn't bother me, but it did. Yeah, I felt a little stupid at first, but then I realized there was nothing wrong with what I said. I took it on the chin, and I had faith that God would use the words I spoke in a positive way. And He did. I received emails and tweets from people who told me how much the documentary encouraged them in their faith. You see, a lightning rod must be willing to be struck by lightning. It hurts, but somebody's got to do it. Saul of Tarsus was also becoming a lightning rod in preparation for the ministry that God would give him.

The Lost Years

During the next several years, Saul went through a null period in his life. One writer simply states, "Paul drops out of history."[44] Up to this point, it seemed that Saul's post-conversion life had nothing to do with proclaiming the gospel before Gentiles, kings, and the children of Israel.

Remember, his first three years as a believer were spent in solitude in the Arabian Desert growing in his faith. When he tried to spread the gospel in Damascus and Jerusalem, he was threatened with death and sent away for his own safety. This

---

[44] John Pollack, *The Apostle: A Life of Paul* (Colorado Springs, CO: Cook Communications Ministries, 1985), 51.

highly trained rabbi-turned-Christian suddenly found himself back in his hometown of Tarsus. This would not be an easy time.

Many believe that during this time he suffered the "loss of all things" that he wrote of in Philippians 3:8.[45] As a trained rabbi, Saul had studied in Jerusalem at the feet of Gamaliel, the most revered rabbi of the day. Not only was Saul a trained rabbi, but he was also the son of a Pharisee (Acts 23:6). He came from a very zealous Jewish family. Many infer that Saul was disinherited during this time and suffered great personal loss.[46] In addition, Saul endured physical punishment for proclaiming the Gospel during those years, as mentioned in 2 Corinthians 11:22–27.[47]

Although he spent his time laboring away in obscurity, Saul remained faithful. While he was alone and forgotten, he held on to the promise that he would proclaim the gospel before Gentiles, kings, and the children of Israel. Exactly how many years Saul spent in Cilicia is up for debate, but for the sake of our timeline, we will go with five years.[48]

Think about it. Saul was not on some fascinating missionary journey. He was not writing scripture. He was in his home region in exile for his own safety. The gospel, however, continued to spread and change cultures. The changes it made in the Gentile

---

[45] MacArthur, 314.

[46] John Phillips, *Exploring Acts, The Phillips Commentary Series* (Grand Rapids, MI: Kregel Publications, 1986), 221.

[47] F. F. Bruce, *Paul: Apostle of the Heart Set Free* (Grand Rapids, MI: William B. Eerdmans, 1977), 127.

[48] Hindson, 158.

world created the need for a man like Saul—a man who could bridge the gap between the Jewish and the Gentile worlds.

The Founder Returns

One of the greatest companies in American history is Apple. Steve Jobs, Steve Wozniak, and Ronald Wayne founded the company on April 1, 1976.[49] Of the three founders, the most notable is Steve Jobs, whose name is synonymous with Apple. However, some may forget that he quit Apple in 1985 when he was stripped of all of his executive power by the board of directors and given the working title of "Global Product Visionary."[50]

Soon after his departure, Jobs founded NeXT and Pixar computer animation studios. These companies became so successful that eleven years after his ignominious departure, Apple bought his new companies for $430 million and appointed him as an advisor.[51]

One year thereafter, Apple made him interim CEO, and the rest is history. Many might assume that Jobs's twelve years of exile were totally unnecessary, but they would be wrong. It seems that

[49] "Apple Inc." *New World Encyclopedia*. Accessed June 23, 2016. http://www.newworldencyclopedia.org/entry/Apple_Inc.

[50] Henry Blodget, "Let's Get One Thing Straight: Apple Had No Choice But to Oust Steve Jobs," *Business Insider*, September 23, 2013. http://www.businessinsider.com/apple-had-no-choice-with-steve-jobs-2013-9.

[51] "Steve Jobs: Timeline," *The Telegraph*. Accessed June 23, 2016. http://www.telegraph.co.uk/technology/steve-jobs/8810045/Steve-Jobs-timeline.html.

those years had a seasoning effect on Jobs. They taught him how to be a great CEO and not just a great computer wizard. Here's how one business writer put it:

> During his time in the wilderness—the 12 years he spent away from the company that became his life's work—Steve learned the skills and discipline that he needed to lead Apple's resurrection. Steve wasn't born with those skills. He *developed* them. And his success in developing them should inspire anyone willing to adopt the simple, powerful goal of getting better every day.[52]

You see, time in exile can make you better if you let it. Saul's years in exile prepared him for a ministry that would change the world.

---

[52] http://www.businessinsider.com/apple-had-no-choice-with-steve-jobs-2013-9.

CHAPTER 6

Returning from Obscurity

Unbeknownst to Saul, his friend Barnabas set out on a quest to find him. Barnabas was overwhelmed; the church in Jerusalem had given him the task to go to Antioch and oversee the explosive growth of the gospel among the Gentiles. Barnabas realized that the task of ministering to this growing Gentile-dominated church was more than he could handle. He needed help. In Barnabas's mind, no one was more qualified to evangelize and to disciple Gentile converts than Saul.[53]

Barnabas traveled to Tarsus to try to find Saul. Scripture says, "Then Barnabas departed for Tarsus to seek Saul" (Acts 11:25). It is interesting that the word translated as "seek" was used to describe how someone would search diligently for a criminal or a fugitive.[54] Barnabas had to hunt Saul down like a private detective.

---

[53] Bruce, 133.

[54] Clinton E. Arnold, *Zondervan Illustrated Bible Backgrounds Commentary*, Volume 2, John, Acts (Grand Rapids, MI: Zondervan, 2002), 318.

When he found him, Barnabas explained how greatly Saul was needed in Antioch, and Saul agreed to join Barnabas in that ministry. Popular Bible teacher Chuck Swindoll summarizes their journey from Tarsus to Antioch as follows: "In that journey with Barnabas to Antioch, the Lord lifted Saul from the shadows of obscurity and placed him back in the action. It was as if the Lord said, 'Now is the time.'"[55]

During his years in exile, Saul's dependence on God greatly increased while his dependence on himself dramatically decreased. Some lessons require time. Saul was ready for the work that God had called him to do.

Time for a Change

Seven years after we planted the church, I knew something needed to change. It seemed like we had hit a wall. We had no building, one staff member (me), and no momentum. Additionally, I was out of gas. So, once again, I was willing to look into a church merger. This time it had to be a merger and not a takeover.

There was a church in our area that was a few years older and a little larger. The pastor was a great guy, and as a matter of fact, our churches had just had a joint baptismal service. I went to talk with my pastor friend about a possible church merger, but before I did so, I sought the counsel of one of my dearest friends. I thought if anyone would give me the right counsel, it was my friend Vince.

---

[55] Swindoll, 88.

When I asked Vince's advice about merging churches, he said, "I thought you should have done it a year ago." That's all I needed. I called the other pastor, and we discussed the merger over lunch.

Believe it or not, within five weeks, our two churches merged into one. We signed over all of our assets, and I became the teaching pastor. It was a God thing. I cannot adequately describe how much I needed this change. I felt like Barnabas had come to get me. I could now see the light at the end of the tunnel, and it was no longer a train.

Back in the Flow

Once in Antioch, Saul assisted in discipling the expanding number of new believers. His task was to help the Gentile converts there grow in their faith. The ministry was so effective that scripture tells us it was at this time in Antioch that believers were first called Christians (Acts 11:26). Some commentators are quick to point out that "Christian" was originally meant as a derogatory term. However, it also attests to the fact that the movement toward Christ was so great that citizens of Antioch needed a new descriptor when identifying those who were flocking to the new faith.[56] The Gentile world came alive with the gospel, and Saul was right in the middle of it.

During this time, there was a famine in Jerusalem, and the church at Antioch collected an offering to help the destitute believers in Judea. The church designated Barnabas and Saul to

---

[56] Arnold, 319.

deliver the aid. This was Saul's second post-conversion visit to Jerusalem, and this time there was no controversy. The people of Jerusalem had either forgotten about him or no longer viewed him as a threat. It had been over a decade since his conversion.

When Barnabas and Saul returned from Jerusalem, they brought a young man named John Mark with them. He would have an interesting role to play as the adventures of Barnabas and Saul unfolded.

Finally!

After their return to Antioch, Barnabas and Saul continued to disciple believers. During one of their worship services, something unexpected happened. The Holy Spirit spoke and said, "Now separate to Me Barnabas and Saul for the work to which I have called them" (Acts 13:2). After a time of fasting and prayer, the church laid hands on these two men and sent them on their first missionary journey.

Noted Bible expositor James Montgomery Boice summarizes Saul's life up to this point:

> Saul has been in the background for a long time. He seems to have faded from sight, at least to the eyes of the people in Jerusalem. Most had forgotten about him. Paul had spent three obscure years in Arabia, had been perhaps seven years in Asia Minor at Tarsus, and now had spent two more years at Antioch. Twelve years! Paul was

getting on into his middle age at this point, and he had not been used much—certainly not in any great pioneer work among Gentiles, which God had told him he would do.[57]

Saul was seasoned and ready for what God called him to do. However, his outlook was not the only thing that changed.

What's in a Name?

Actor Ramon Estevez altered his name to Martin Sheen because he felt that his Hispanic ancestry made it harder for him to get a job. Estevez came up with his new name by combining the last names of the casting director who gave him his first big break with the last name of the popular Catholic televangelist Archbishop Fulton J. Sheen.[58]

In Acts 13:9 we are told in almost an offhanded way that Saul was also known as Paul. As a Hellenized Jew, Saul had a Hebrew name as well as a Roman name.[59] Just as his Jewish name, Saul, communicated his connection with Israel's first king, so his Roman name, Paul, communicated his connection with the larger Greco-Roman world.[60]

---

[57] James Montgomery Boice, *Acts* (Grand Rapids, MI: Baker Books, 2002), 232.

[58] Rose Pacatte, *Martin Sheen: A Pilgrim on the Way* (Collegeville, MN: Liturgical Press, 2015), 6.

[59] John B. Polhill, *New American Commentary: Acts* (Nashville, TN, Broadman Press, 1992), 295.

[60] Frank E. Gaebelein, *The Expositor's Bible Commentary: John–Acts*, Vol. 9 (Grand Rapids, MI: Zondervan Publishing, 1981), 420.

In addition, after this point in the book of Acts, we no longer hear of Barnabas and Saul, but instead of Paul and Barnabas.

As the missionary duo blazed a trail into the heart of Gentile territory, not only did Saul's name change, but he also became the acknowledged leader of this expedition in spreading the gospel.[61] Saul's mission had finally come to fruition. He was now the apostle Paul, and as such, he would plant churches all throughout the Gentile world. This man of faith would share Christ with dignitaries such as King Agrippa, Governors Festus and Felix, and even the emperor of Rome. Additionally, he would give a defense of the gospel before the ruling Jewish council known as the Sanhedrin as well as an angry Jewish mob in Jerusalem. Finally, he would solidify his legacy by authoring approximately one-third of the New Testament. God's word came true. It just took time.

Tying up Loose Ends

When I resigned from the church, a lot of unfortunate things were said about me. To say I was heartbroken would be a great understatement. It was unfortunate because I had a great relationship with the vast majority of the church members. However, the church operated with a polity that was ripe for conflict and failure.

Over the years, it bothered me that there was a place that I felt like I could not go back to. This meant that when there was a funeral, I did not feel like I could attend. I felt like my

---

[61] Polhill, 295.

presence would be a distraction. But all of that changed in a most unexpected way.

My youngest daughter, Masey, is an actress. She was blessed to play the lead role of Rachel Joy Scott in the movie *I'm Not Ashamed*. Because the movie was faith-based, many churches bought out theaters to watch it. The church I left bought out one of the theater rooms at our local theater, and it just so happened that we went to see the movie on the same night.

As we entered the theater at the mall, I saw many of our former church members. It was like nothing had ever happened. Everyone was nice, and they had even scheduled Masey to film an interview for a nationwide ministry at the church. The pastor asked if I would like to come with Masey for the interview. Initially, I declined the invitation, but the next morning I woke up and felt that the Lord was telling me that I had to go. So, I went with my daughter to the interview at the church that I had resigned from nine years earlier.

When we arrived, it was a surreal experience. The last service that I attended there had been my resignation. Admittedly, I was a little nervous as to how everything would turn out. To my surprise, the pastor asked me if I would come forward at the end of the interview and close the service with prayer. I wasn't expecting such a request, but I agreed to do it.

As I sat listening to my daughter talk about the movie, I felt the Lord speak to my heart and tell me that when I prayed I needed to ask Him to bless the church. Remember, this is the church from which I resigned. This is the church that had members who had slandered me. However, time has a way of healing all wounds.

When the pastor called me up, I prayed a brief prayer and asked God to bless the church. My daughter said that when I prayed, she could feel a collective sigh leave the room. It's like something was released. Afterward, I had great conversations with members, and when I left, I could close a chapter in my life. Now I felt like I could go back and go forward.

Putting It All Together

Saul had a lot in his past that he had to overcome. God completely changed his life and gave him an incredible purpose. He was to share the gospel with Gentiles, kings, and the children of Israel. However, he had to wait over ten years before his life got on track with what Jesus told him he would do.

Early on it seemed as though every time he got cranked up with the gospel, he would get shut down. He got shut down in Damascus and then in Jerusalem. For his own safety, he was sent into exile to his home region for five or more years. He also had to deal with people who did not believe his sincerity. Had it not been for Barnabas, the church in Jerusalem would have left him out in the cold.

After Saul's amazing conversion experience and call to the ministry, nothing greatly significant happened for the following several years. He labored away in Cilicia and suffered loss, both physically and relationally.

Can you take it when your career path leads you into a time of obscurity? Can you stay the course when others see you as a vestige of the past?

Saul's future depended on events beyond his control. Two churches made him leave for his own safety. He wasn't asked to teach or to exercise any form of leadership. Instead, he was viewed as a hazard that needed to get out of town.

As he labored year after year in Cilicia, Saul had no way of knowing that a unique situation was being created for him in the church at Antioch. This Gentile-dominated church was an ideal fit for the calling and gifts that Saul possessed. When the time was right, God put it into the heart of Barnabas to bring Saul to Antioch. He was the man for the job.

Do you believe that God has uniquely equipped you to build His kingdom here on earth? Are you willing to live in obscurity until God puts you in a place uniquely suited for you?

Dangerous Disappointment

Men have to guard against disappointment during times of testing. Dwelling on disappointment has a way of messing with how you think. Take, for instance, the circumstances surrounding the writing of the book of Malachi in the Old Testament.

Malachi was the last prophet in the Old Testament. After Malachi, there would be a silence of approximately four hundred years before another prophet, John the Baptist, would burst onto the scene. In his prophetic role, Malachi addressed issues such as divorce, robbing God, and social justice.

The Jewish people in Malachi's day were disillusioned. In the past one hundred years, the Jews had returned from captivity, Zerubbabel had rebuilt the temple, Ezra had reinstated the law, and Nehemiah had rebuilt the wall around Jerusalem.

It seemed like the stage was being set for something really big to happen. However, the Jews found themselves still under Persian rule. Their crops were failing, and their futures looked bleak. Life was not turning out the way they thought it would. There was no sign of a Messiah.

In their disappointment, they started to make accusations against God. They said, "Everyone who does evil is good in the sight of the Lord, And He delights in them. It is useless to serve God; What profit is it that we have kept His ordinance, And that we have walked as mourners Before the Lord of hosts?" (Malachi 2:17; 3:14). This distortion would begin to have a devastating impact upon their behavior.

Disappointment can be dangerous when we allow it to distort our view of God. As we develop this emotionally driven theology, our behavior begins to change. This change is never good. So, if you are struggling with disappointment, always remember to maintain a biblical understanding of God's character. He does not change.

Malachi reminds the people of this fact in Malachi 3:6 when he writes, "For I am the Lord, I do not change." Our circumstances do not change who God is. He is the same when life is bad as He is when life is good. Use sound theology to interpret your circumstances. Don't develop your theology from your circumstances. God is good, and God is great. He does not change!

CONCLUSION

My hope is that you feel as though you can make it now. You are not alone. You are not the only one who has experienced a downturn of fortune. Life is full of twists and turns, and unless the Lord returns before our lives are over, none of us will get out of here alive. We will all suffer the ultimate downturn known as death. However, don't live your life not to die. Live your life to win. Isn't that what the Bible says? "Do you not know that those who run in a race all run, but one receives the prize? Run in such a way that you may obtain it" (1 Cor. 9:24). It's like what William Wallace said before his torturous death in *Braveheart*: "Every man dies. Not every man really lives."[62] Live with all you've got, even when it seems as though you are in the wilderness. Don't give up, and don't give in. Your life is important.

If I had given up, I would have missed so many wonderful things that the Lord did not only in my life but also in the lives of others. I got to experience God's provision and providence in ways that I would have never chosen, but I wouldn't give anything for.

---

[62] www.imdb.com/title/tt0112573/quotes.

When we started the new church, the leadership team paid me the same salary I made at the church I resigned. I didn't ask for it; that is what they decided to do. Also, after ten years, our family emerged debt free. God provided in ways that far exceeded our imagination. I got to be good friends with some of the greatest men I have ever known, who encouraged me when I was down. They reminded me of God's call on my life, and they loved my family. I could not have asked for a better support system.

When we merged churches, my oldest son met a godly young lady from the other church who became his wife. Not only did we merge churches, but we also merged families. My oldest daughter married a wonderful Christian man, and they have given us our first grandchild. Our youngest daughter became an up-and-coming actress, and our youngest son is a stout football player for a great high school.

In some ways, I feel like Caleb of the Old Testament. After being denied entry into the Promised Land for forty years because of the bad report given to Moses by the ten faithless spies, this man of faith did not lose his vim or vigor. After forty years, he still had his eyes on the prize. Listen to these words that he spoke to Joshua, Israel's new leader:

> As yet I am as strong this day as on the day that Moses sent me; just as my strength was then, so now is my strength for war, both for going out and for coming in. Now therefore, give me this mountain of which the Lord spoke in that day; for you heard in that day how the Anakim were

there, and that the cities were great and fortified.
It may be that the Lord will be with me, and I
shall be able to drive them out as the Lord said.
(Joshua 14:11–12)

The Anakim were giants, and Caleb still wanted to go after them. There was some unfinished business he needed to tend to. Even at eighty-five years of age, he still wanted to walk by faith and do great things for God. His wilderness experience had not diminished his faith.

You too can be like Caleb. You can emerge from your wilderness experience with a vibrant faith. Sure, you may have a lot to overcome, but didn't Joseph, David, and Saul? Joseph summarized his ordeal by saying, "You meant evil against me; but God meant it for good, in order to bring it about as it is this day, to save many people alive" (Gen. 50:20). Against incredible forces arrayed in his life, David wrote, "When I cry out to You, then my enemies will turn back; This I know, because God is for me" (Psalm 56:9). In his later years, Saul/Paul wrote to believers in Philippi saying, "being confident of this very thing, that He who has begun a good work in you will complete it until the day of Jesus Christ" (Phil. 1:6). Also, the words that he communicated to the church in Rome summarize perfectly what this little book has been about: "And we know that all things work together for good to those who love God, to those who are the called according to His purpose. For whom He foreknew, He also predestined to be conformed to the image of His Son" (Rom. 8:28–29).

If your wilderness experience conforms you to the image of Christ, then you are connected to God's purpose. God is working in your life; He may just be working in a way that you would not have chosen. Take heart. Dig deep. Run to win!

Printed in the United States
By Bookmasters